Agnes

I have tampered with the divine plan.

by
TONY COCHRAN

**Andrews McMeel
Publishing**

Kansas City

Agnes is syndicated by Creators Syndicate. For information, write Creators Syndicate, 5777 W. Century Blvd., Suite 700, Los Angeles, California 90045.

05 06 07 08 09 BBG 10 9 8 7 6 5 4 3 2 1

ISBN: 0-7407-5000-3

Library of Congress Control Number: 2004112542

Agnes would like to visit you every day. Please contact your local newspaper to add Agnes to the daily and Sunday comics pages if she is not already there. She says, "Thanks!"

—— **ATTENTION: SCHOOLS AND BUSINESSES** ——

Andrews McMeel books are available at quantity discounts with bulk purchase for educational, business, or sales promotional use. For information, please write to: Special Sales Department, Andrews McMeel Publishing, 4520 Main Street, Kansas City, Missouri 64111.

**For Mom and Dad.
It's your fault I'm like this.**

Dear Miss Becherich,

I am sorry for not replying to your note sooner. I only just found it last night all wadded up in the toe of Agnes's sock. I always check her socks carefully before I launder them because I simply can not afford to have another lump of jujubes or gummy bears jam the pump in the washing machine again. Agnes claims she puts them there because "the school is rife with roving bands of vagabond monkeys who pilfer willy nilly from the lockers with no regard for the sanctity of rightful ownership." I have my doubts.

I apologize that her homework is not being completed in a timely and conscientious manner but, despite what she has told you, WE DO HAVE ACCESS TO ELECTRICITY AND I AM NOT A ROGUE C.I.A. OPERATIVE WHO ONLY "BLOWS INTO TOWN OCCASIONALLY TO CHECK HER MAIL AND GRAB A QUICK SHAVE."

As for the other matter, I try to raise Agnes with respect for the church. But I have never ONCE referred to her math book as "Satan's manuscript" nor told her that using pencils or pens was "like grabbing the horns of the devil himself!"

I am looking forward to meeting you on Parents' night next week.

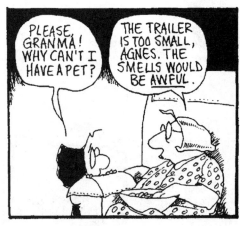

Agnes
by TONY COCHRAN

I'LL GIVE THEM ANOTHER FORTY MINUTES.

GOOD MORNING, GRANMA. I HAVE FOR YOU THE OBLIGATORY ODD-COLORED BOILED CHICKEN EGG THAT SYMBOLIZES EASTER LOVE.

SNORKK......

...AND NOW, I WILL SERENADE YOU WITH EASTER CAROLS. THIS FIRST DITTY IS AN OLD STANDBY ABOUT A SMALL, CONFUSED GIRL... SHE ATTEMPTS TO GAIN POPULARITY IN A TOWN'S EASTER RITUAL BY ADORNING HER HAND-ME-DOWN HAT WITH VARIOUS FLORA.

?HMMPH?

OF COURSE, IN MY VERSION, THE TRUE SPIRIT OF THE SEASON EMERGES AS SHE ABANDONS THE PARADE DOWN THE MEAN STREETS TO DO MISSION WORK AMONG THE BAG PEOPLE.

AM I DREAMING, OR IS THERE A RABBIT ON MY STOMACH?

T. COCHRAN

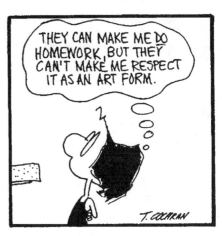

23

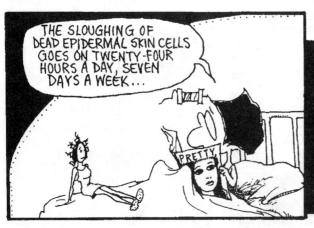

Agnes
by TONY COCHRAN

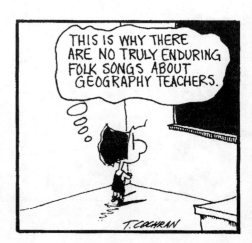

35

Agnes
by TONY COCHRAN

HERE YOU GO, YOU SORRY, SOGGY DUCKS! OLD, STALE BREAD! POP-TART SHARDS! CAST-OFF CRACKERS!

UH-OH! ALL GONE! GO SNORK DOWN SOME WOUNDED MINNOWS... YOUR FREE RIDE'S OVER!

NOW WHAT?

NOW WE SIT BACK AND ENJOY THE "INNER GLOW" THAT COMES FROM PERFORMING GOOD WORKS.

I'M NOT GLOWING.

ME, EITHER. WE'LL WAIT UNTIL THEY ARE HUNGRIER NEXT TIME.

T. COCHRAN

Agnes
by
TONY COCHRAN

The Sickly Trees by Agnes

Standing crooked and gnarly,
Their old bark sloughing off,
If you're quiet in the woods,
You can hear sick trees cough.

TREES DON'T COUGH, AGNES.

AHEM!..

Heaving and gagging,
They choke on their sap,
Then, eyes reddened with effort,
They take a short nap.

WELL, THERE AGAIN, AGNES, TREES DON'T HAVE EYES.

ARE WE IN AGREEMENT, HOWEVER, THAT TREES DO NAP OCCASIONALLY? HMMM?

NO ONE KNOWS IF TREES TAKE NAPS.

The Napping Trees by Agnes

SIGH... THERE WON'T BE AS MUCH CLAMOR FOR THE MOVIE RIGHTS.

T. COCHRAN

Agnes

by
TONY COCHRAN

WHAT HAVE YOU FOUND, TROUT?

A SPIDER WITH ONLY TWO LEGS! HE KEEPS WALKIN' IN A CIRCLE, OVER AND OVER!

I'M GONNA WATCH HIM AND SEE HOW LONG IT TAKES FOR HIM TO GET ALL DIZZY AND FALL DOWN!

WAIT... IF HIS BELLY IS ALREADY DRAGGING ON THE GROUND, HOW WILL WE KNOW WHEN HE'S FALLEN?

I IMAGINE THERE WILL BE A QUITE AUDIBLE SIGH OF EXASPERATION.

T. COCHRAN

GRANMA? WHO AM I? WHAT WILL BECOME OF ME? HOW WILL I FIND MY PATH TO THE FUTURE?

YOU DON'T HAVE TO FIND A PATH TO YOUR FUTURE. IT REACHES UP AND SLAPS YOU LIKE A COLD, DEAD FISH ON THE SECOND TUESDAY OF EVERY MONTH.

T. COCHRAN

THE JOURNAL ENTRIES GET A LITTLE BLUNT ON PAYDAYS.

IF PEOPLE DREAM OF FLYING, WHAT DO BIRDS DREAM?

THEY DREAM OF LOPING ACROSS THAT FIELD WITH THEIR FLANKS GLISTENING LIKE SWEATY PONIES.

OH?

AND I BET THEY DREAM OF KISSING WITH MALLEABLE MOUTHS.

T. COCHRAN

I WISH ANXIETY HAD BEEN LEFT OUT OF THE DIVINE PLAN.

HUH?

I CAN'T THINK OF A SINGLE GOOD USE FOR IT. IT'S LIKE A HORRID, HUNGRY BUG.

RELENTLESSLY, IT CRAWLS UP AND DOWN MY TENDER ABDOMEN, POKING AND PRODDING WITH PRICKLY PINCERS AND ITS NEEDLE-LIKE LITTLE BEETLE FEET, SEARCHING FOR SUSTENANCE.

MAYBE IF YOU FEED IT, IT WILL GO AWAY.

IT'S ALREADY CHOWED DOWN MOST OF MY CAREFREE YOUTH.

T. COCHRAN

Agnes

by TONY COCHRAN

OH YES!

NOW TO FIND A CAPTURED AUDIENCE.

TROUT, I HAVE A NEW POEM ABOUT LIFE'S PLIGHT.

AGNES... WE'RE FRIENDS, RIGHT? AND FRIENDS SHOULD SET FRIENDS STRAIGHT.

I KNOW YOU HAVE THIS CUTE, INNOCENT DREAM OF HITTING IT BIG WITH YOUR POETRY, BUT YOUR POETRY IS REALLY, REALLY BAD.

FINE, LITTLE MISS CRITIC! I'M LEAVING! BUT I WILL HAVE YOU KNOW, MY POETRY IS NOT JUST SOME INNOCENT DREAM!

IT'S MORE OF A SCAM.

Agnes

by TONY COCHRAN

Dear Mr. Brokaw
Dear Mr. Rather
Dear Mr. Philbin

Dear Mr. Jennings,
I have decided to embark down the road to becoming a network anchor person. A road I know will be littered with pitfalls. obstacles.

are there any words of advice you would share with me, to facilitate my realization of this, my ultimate goal?

T COCHRAN

also, are you ever tempted to make stuff up?... just for a hoot?

IT WOULD BE NICE TO KNOW IF WE ARE BATTLING THE SAME DEMONS.

61

65

Agnes
by TONY COCHRAN

AGNES, DO YOU THINK BOYS WILL EVER BECOME AN ISSUE BETWEEN US?

ABSURD. BOYS ARE ONLY A CRUDE LIFE-FORM... MERE CURIOSITIES SENT HERE TO CLOUD UP THE REAL PURPOSE OF EXISTENCE.

FOR INSTANCE... THAT CLOD OVER THERE... MAKING ODD NOISES WITH HIS ARMPIT. HE'S REALLY, REALLY TRYING TO BE FUNNY, BUT HE IS DEVOID OF ANY WIT. HE IS ADDING NOTHING TO OUR LIVES. HOW COULD HE POSSIBLY ALTER OUR FRIENDSHIP?

I THINK HE'S FUNNY! I'M GOING TO GO WATCH!

SO... OUR FIRST FORK IN THE ROAD TURNED OUT TO BE AN ARMPIT.

T. COCHRAN

Agnes

by
TONY COCHRAN

I'M FAIRLY CONTENT WITH MY CURRENT FAME, BUT I WOULD LIKE TO BREAK THROUGH TO THE NEXT LEVEL.

YOU'RE NOT FAMOUS.

WELL... NOT FAMOUS IN THE TRUEST SENSE OF THE WORD, BUT I DO ENJOY A BIT OF REGIONAL POPULARITY.

NO... ACTUALLY, YOU DON'T.

NOT POPULAR IN THE BROADEST USE OF THE WORD, BUT I AM SORT OF A LOCAL HERO.

NO, YOU'RE NOT.

I AM THE CENTER HUB IN A LARGE CIRCLE OF FRIENDS?

NOT REALLY,... THERE'S JUST ME, AND I HAVE TO GO HOME AND DO THE LAUNDRY.

IT'S JUST AS WELL... HER CONSTANT ADULATION GETS TEDIOUS AFTER AWHILE.

T COCHRAN

Agnes

by TONY COCHRAN

PRETTY

AGNES, WHAT DO YOU WANT TO BE WHEN YOU GROW UP?

A FORENSIC PATHOLOGIST FOR INTERPOL. PREFERABLY WITH A HOME-BASE SUITE OF OFFICES ON THE RIVIERA.

PRETTY
YOU

I WANT TO PILOT ONE OF THOSE SOFT-SERVE ICE CREAM MACHINES. I WOULD POLISH IT EVERY NIGHT. ...AND ALL THE KIDS WILL YELL, "HEY, ICE CREAM LADY!"

THIS MEANS WE WILL BE IN DIFFERENT BOWLING LEAGUES, RIGHT?

T. COCHRAN

My Summer Vacation by Agnes
This summer did not turn out as I had planned.

I accomplished absolutely nothing that was noteworthy or remarkable.

a theme I would love to continue well into the last paragraph of this composition.

This summer, we planted a new bush. it felt good to get back to the earth.

We dug a hole, put the bush in the hole, watered it, mulched it, and watched it die a slow, agonizing death.

Landscaping is a real crapshoot.

THE OLD TRUCK IS RUNNING A LITTLE ROUGH!

DID YOU RE-GAP THE PLUG ON THE NUMBER TWO CYLINDER?

THE GAP WAS FINE.

THEN I SUSPECT THE IGNITION WIRES MAY BE ARCING. IT'S DAMP TODAY.

MOST KIDS ONLY HAVE TO REMEMBER THEIR BOOTS WHEN IT RAINS.

I WISH I WAS A PRINCESS... PEOPLE WOULD HAVE TO LIKE ME.

LIKE IT MAKES ANY DIFFERENCE.

WOULD IT MAKE YOU LIKE ME ANY BETTER IF I WAS A PRINCESS?

WELL?

WOULD YOU HAVE A ROYAL PONY?

WELL, I HANDLED THAT ROUND OF PEER MOCKERY QUITE HANDILY!

THEIR LITTLE CLIQUE NOW HAS A BIT OF RELUCTANT RESPECT FOR ME... AT LEAST UNTIL THREE O'CLOCK.

WHAT HAPPENS AT THREE O'CLOCK?

I'VE INVITED THEM OVER TO HELP ME HERD MY PONIES.

AGNES, YOU DON'T HAVE A HERD OF PONIES!

NO... BUT I DO HAVE ALMOST TWO HOURS OF BEING TREATED AS IF I DO.

BUT WHEN THEY GET TO THE TRAILER PARK AND FIND OUT THAT YOU JUST MADE IT UP, THEY'LL BE EVEN NASTIER!

TWO HOURS, TROUT. I'M SURE A PONY OR TWO WILL SHOW UP IN TWO HOURS!

IN ALL MY YEARS AT THIS SCHOOL, I'VE NEVER SEEN A PONY IN FIFTH PERIOD,

BECAUSE YOU ARE ALWAYS FOCUSED ON THE FLOOR SHOW.

Agnes
by
TONY COCHRAN

FWOOOP...
FWOPPA!
FWIP!
FWIP!
FWIP-FWOP!
FWIP
FFWIP!
FWIPPA!

PULL UP YOUR SOCKS, AGNES. THEY'RE FLOPPING AROUND LIKE DEAD SNAKES.

MY TOES GET VERY DEPRESSED WHEN THEY ARE GIRDLED TIGHTLY IN HOSIERY.

YOUR TOES GET DEPRESSED?

YES... AND IF I HAVE LEARNED ANYTHING IN LIFE, IT'S KEEP YOUR FEET DIGITS HAPPY.

AS I ALWAYS SAY, "UNSWADDLE THOU TOES, AND FOREVER THEY WILL THANKETH THEE."

T. COCHRAN

I HAVE NEVER HEARD YOU SAY THAT.

WELL... IT'S NOT SOMETHING I SAY VERY LOUDLY.

81

Agnes

by TONY COCHRAN

Agnes
by
TONY COCHRAN

SIGH... I'VE DONE THIS ALL BEFORE... THE ABBREVIATED NIGHT'S SLEEP... THE QUICKLY GOBBLED BREAKFAST... THE MINDLESS TREK TO SCHOOL.

I AM SYSYPHUS. DOOMED TO PUSH THE BOULDER OF MY DAY TO THE CREST OF THE HILL, ONLY TO HAVE IT ROLL DOWN AGAIN. THERE IS NO END TO THE PUSHING, PUSHING, PUSHING.

HEY AGNES! DID YOU KNOW THAT IF I PINCH MY NOSE TIGHT, AND BLOW REAL HARD, MY EARS WHISTLE?!

FFFFWEEEEP!

SOME ARE OBVIOUSLY ONLY PUSHING WITH ONE HAND.

FWEEP! FWEEEP! FWEEEEP

T. COCHRAN

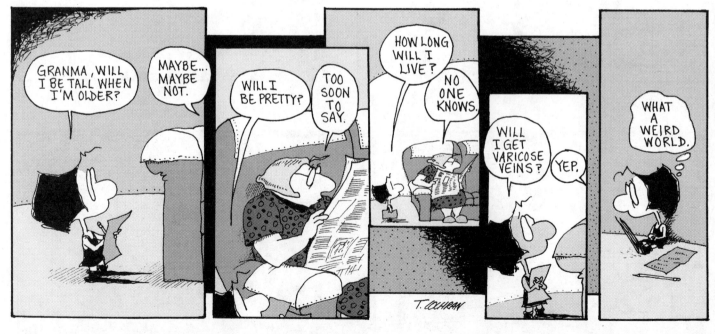

Agnes

by
TONY COCHRAN

OKAY... I CLEARED MY SHARE. IT'S YOUR TURN TO MAN THE SHOVEL.

...AND IT'S MY TURN TO BE THE BOSS!

HEH HEH.. ON THE CONTRARY, MY STURDY LABORER.. SEEMS WE ARE WAY, <u>WAY</u> OVER BUDGET ON THIS PROJECT... SHIFT CHANGES WILL NOT BE APPROVED.

IT'S NOT A SHIFT CHANGE... IT'S A <u>BOSS</u> CHANGE!

TSK... AIR YOUR GRIEVANCE AT THE NEXT UNION MEETING. I HAVE HOT COCOA TO QUAFF.

MAY AS WELL ADD UNAUTHORIZED USE OF CITY EQUIPMENT TO THE LIST.

Dear Oprah,
My Granma is a certifiable mess.

WHEW!... THAT'S PRETTY COLD, AGNES.

DO YOU THINK OPRAH WOULD WASTE NATIONAL AIR TIME TO MERELY TWEEZE A BUSHY EYEBROW OR TWO? NO! WE HAVE TO TUG SOME SERIOUS HEARTSTRINGS HERE!

YOU WANT THAT PICTURE OF YOUR GRANMA CHANGING BANDAGES AFTER HER HAMMER TOE SURGERY?

IF I COULD BE SURE OPRAH DIDN'T PERUSE THESE OVER LUNCH.

Dear Oprah,
My Granma doesn't look so good.
Her body is a tad misshapen, and gravity has tugged on her face relentlessly.

...in her favor, she has no visible tattoo, and is amazingly comfortable with her nose girth.

I'M SURE THEY FACTOR IN COST EFFECTIVENESS.

Here is a picture of my Granma. I had to snap it on the sly. She would be livid if she knew I was seeking handouts.

I had to hide in the hamper quite awhile. The aroma of damp socks lingered on me for days!

She's only shiny because she is in the shower. Her natural patina is much duller.

OPRAH'S COSMETIC EXPERTS WILL APPRECIATE THE HEADS UP.

126